Lerner SPORTS

SPORTS TEAM SMACKDOWN

BOSTON CELTICS VS. LOS ANGELES LAKERS

RIVAL RUMBLE

JOSH ANDERSON

Lerner Publications ◆ Minneapolis

To Leo: I can't wait to see the many chapters of your bright future.

Stats in this book are accurate through the 2024–2025 NBA regular season.

Lerner Publications Company
An imprint of Lerner Publishing Group, Inc.
241 First Avenue North
Minneapolis, MN 55401 USA

For reading levels and more information, look up this title at www.lernerbooks.com.

Main body text set in Aptifer Sans LT Pro.
Typeface provided by Linotype AG.

Library of Congress Cataloging-in-Publication Data

Names: Anderson, Josh author
Title: Boston Celtics vs. Los Angeles Lakers : rival rumble / Josh Anderson.
Other titles: Boston Celtics versus Los Angeles Lakers
Description: Minneapolis, MN : Lerner Publications, [2026] | Series: Sports team smackdown (Lerner sports) | Includes bibliographical references and index. | Audience: Ages 7–11 | Audience: Grades 2–3 | Summary: "The Boston Celtics and Los Angeles Lakers have the best rivalry in the NBA. The teams have faced off in the NBA Finals 12 times, and no other teams have won more championships"—Provided by publisher.
Identifiers: LCCN 2025014135 (print) | LCCN 2025014136 (ebook) | ISBN 9798765689493 library binding | ISBN 9798348029357 paperback | ISBN 9798765699027 epub
Subjects: LCSH: Basketball teams—United States—Juvenile literature | Boston Celtics (Basketball team)—Juvenile literature | Los Angeles Lakers (Basketball team)—Juvenile literature | Sports rivalries—United States—Juvenile literature | National Basketball Association—Juvenile literature
Classification: LCC GV885.1 .A54 2026 (print) | LCC GV885.1 (ebook) | DDC 796.323—dc23/eng/20250602

LC record available at https://lccn.loc.gov/2025014135
LC ebook record available at https://lccn.loc.gov/202501413

Manufactured in the United States of America
1 – CG – 12/15/25

TABLE OF CONTENTS

INTRODUCTION

FISHER'S BIG SHOT

The Los Angeles Lakers were playing their biggest rivals in the 2010 National Basketball Association (NBA) Finals. It was the 12th time the Lakers and the Boston Celtics had played in the Finals. After trailing for most of Game 7, the Lakers had come back to make it a close game in the final quarter. The Celtics led 64–61.

With around six minutes left to play, Lakers star Kobe Bryant held the ball outside the three-point line. Bryant saw his high-scoring teammate Pau Gasol close to the basket. Bryant passed the ball to Gasol.

Derek Fisher's three-point shot kept the Lakers alive during Game 7 of the 2010 Finals.

With his back to a Celtics defender, Gasol dribbled toward the basket. When he looked up, Gasol saw teammate Derek Fisher open near the three-point line. Gasol passed Fisher the ball.

Fisher was not one of the Lakers' top scorers. But he often came through for the team in big moments. Fisher launched a three-point shot over Celtics guard Rajon Rondo. The ball went through the hoop, tying the game 64–64. Moments later, Bryant hit two free throws and a jump shot to put the Lakers ahead for good.

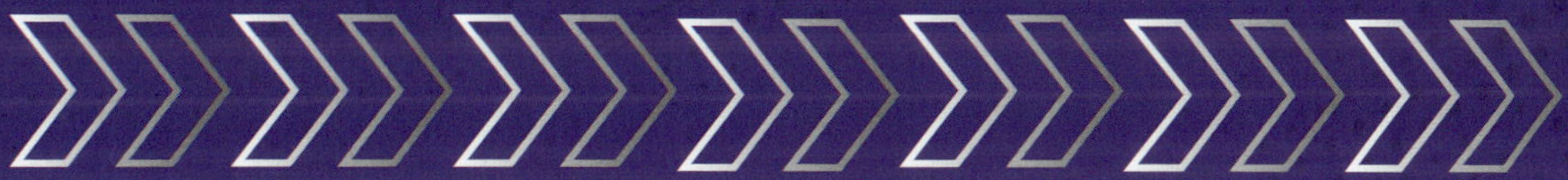

FAST FACTS

- The Celtics have won the NBA title 18 times, while the Lakers have won 17 times.
- The teams last met in the NBA Finals in 2010, with the Lakers coming out on top.
- Lakers star Kareem Abdul-Jabbar holds the NBA record with six career Most Valuable Player (MVP) awards.
- The Lakers won five NBA titles during the 1980s.

The Lakers went on to win 83–79. They earned their 16th NBA championship. Los Angeles won another title in 2020, giving them 17 all-time.

For a few years, both the Lakers and Celtics had 17 championships. But in 2024, Boston earned their 18th title, giving them the slight edge—for now. The Lakers and Celtics have won more NBA titles than any other teams in the league. They have one of the greatest rivalries in all of sports. But which team is best? Let the smackdown begin!

Paul Pierce (left) battles Ron Artest during the 2010 NBA Finals.

SMACKDOWN!

CHAPTER 1

Red Auerbach (left) won nine NBA titles as head coach of the Celtics and seven more as Boston's general manager.

TITLE-WINNING TEAMS

The Celtics began play in 1946. They were one of eight teams in the Basketball Association of America (BAA). In 1949, the BAA joined with another league to form the NBA. Boston won their first title behind coach Red Auerbach in 1957.

Boston's team in the 1950s and 1960s included some of the best players in NBA history. Guards Bob Cousy and Bill Sharman teamed with forward Tom Heinsohn and center Bill Russell to dominate the game. From 1957 to 1969, the Celtics won 11 NBA titles. This included eight titles in a row from 1959 to 1966, the longest title streak in league history. Seven of the Celtics' 11 titles during this time were victories over the Lakers.

Boston continued to be one of the league's strongest teams throughout the 1970s and 1980s. They won five NBA titles during this time. In the 1980s, the rivalry between Celtics star Larry Bird and Lakers star Magic Johnson helped make both players popular with sports fans. The rivalry between Boston and Los Angeles and their star players helped draw more fans to the NBA.

Boston guard Sam Jones dribbles to the basket during a 1965 game between the Celtics and the Philadelphia 76ers.

Since beating the Houston Rockets in the 1986 NBA Finals, the Celtics have won only two titles. One came in 2008 after defeating the Lakers in the Finals. The other was in 2024 when Boston beat the Dallas Mavericks.

In 1947, the National Basketball League's Detroit Gems moved to Minneapolis, Minnesota, and became the Minneapolis Lakers. They joined the NBA in 1949. The Lakers won the NBA Finals in five of the team's first six seasons. During that time, the Lakers had one of the game's first big stars, center George Mikan.

The Lakers moved to Los Angeles, California, in 1960. They played in seven NBA Finals between 1962 and 1970 but lost each time. Six of those losses were to the Celtics. Finally, the Lakers won the title again in 1972 after defeating the New York Knicks in the Finals.

Larry Bird was also an excellent free throw shooter. He made 3,960 of his 4,471 attempted free throws for the Celtics.

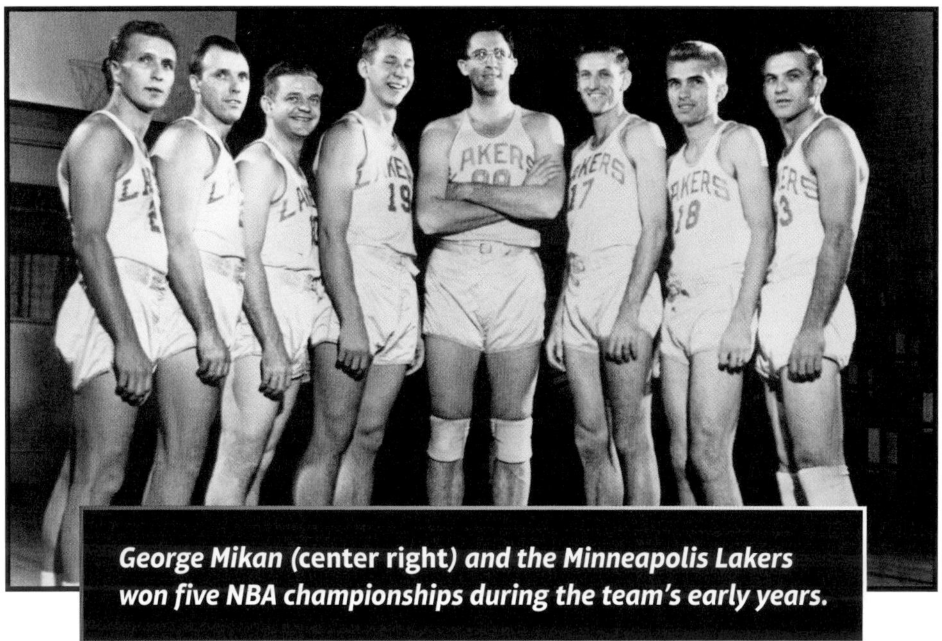

George Mikan (center right) and the Minneapolis Lakers won five NBA championships during the team's early years.

The Lakers' most memorable era came during the 1980s. Nicknamed Showtime because of their fast and exciting playing style, the Lakers dominated the decade. From 1980 to 1988, the Lakers won five titles with legends Kareem Abdul-Jabbar and Earvin "Magic" Johnson. Coach Pat Riley was the Lakers' head coach during four of those title-winning seasons. Two of their NBA Finals victories during that time were against the Celtics.

The Lakers were dominant again from 2000 to 2010. The team played in seven NBA Finals and won five of them. The Lakers had two of the NBA's biggest stars. Center Shaquille O'Neal was one of the biggest and strongest men ever to play the game.

Kobe Bryant was the face of the Lakers for 20 years.

Bryant (left) and Shaquille O'Neal (right) led the Lakers to three NBA titles in the early 2000s.

Guard Kobe Bryant could score from anywhere on the court and thrilled fans with his high-flying moves. O'Neal and Bryant played together for the Lakers from 1996 until O'Neal left the team in 2004.

The Lakers' most recent title came in 2020. That year, superstar LeBron James led the team to victory over the Miami Heat in the Finals. With the Celtics near the top of the league and the Lakers often one of the NBA's best, it's only a matter of time before the teams meet in the Finals again.

CHECK IT OUT

Celtics coach Red Auerbach led Boston to the championship nine times between 1950 and 1966.

CHAPTER 2

The Celtics' Game 7 victory against the Lakers during the 1962 Finals is one of Boston's most memorable moments.

AMAZING MOMENTS

Both the Celtics and Lakers have had many incredible moments on the court. There have only been two seasons in NBA history that neither team made it to the playoffs. Some of the teams' most memorable events have been when the Celtics and Lakers played against each other.

Game 7 of the 1962 Finals could have ended with a Lakers victory. With five seconds left and the game tied, Lakers guard Frank Selvy missed a shot that would have won the game.

Instead, the game went to overtime, and the Celtics won 110–107. Celtics legend Bill Russell's performance in the game was one of the best in league history. He finished with 30 points and 40 rebounds to lead the Celtics to victory.

The Lakers set an NBA record with 69 wins during the 1971–1972 season. Although that record has been broken, another record set during that historic season has not. On their way to winning the championship in 1972, the Lakers won an incredible 33 games in a row. No other team has done that.

Lakers star Wilt Chamberlain shoots over Jim Fox of the Chicago Bulls in a 1971 game.

Kareem Abdul-Jabbar (right) guards Boston's Bill Walton during the 1985 NBA Finals.

The 1984 NBA title came down to the last minute of Game 7. The series was the first time rivals Larry Bird and Magic Johnson had faced off in the NBA Finals. Johnson dribbled down the court, hoping to pull the Lakers within one point. But before he could take a shot, Celtics center Robert Parish knocked the ball from Johnson's hands.

Parish's defensive play sealed the victory for Boston. It was the eighth time the teams had met in the Finals. All eight had gone to the Celtics.

The Celtics and Lakers met again in the 1985 Finals. A 148–114 Celtics victory in Game 1 was called the Memorial Day

CHECK IT OUT

Ten Lakers and Celtics players and coaches from the 1984 and 1985 NBA Finals are members of the Basketball Hall of Fame.

Massacre by fans. It looked like the Celtics would defeat Los Angeles for a ninth time. But the Lakers managed to win the series in six games, earning their first Finals victory over their Boston rivals.

In 1986, the NBA introduced a three-point contest to take place during the weekend of the All-Star game. Competing against other top shooters, Larry Bird won the contest in 1986 and 1987. He looked like he might not win again in 1988 after missing many of his early shots. He needed to beat a score of 15 in the Final. As the clock ticked under 10 seconds, Bird was stuck on 13 baskets. With three seconds remaining,

Larry Bird (pictured) and Craig Hodges are tied for the most NBA three-point contest wins with three.

Kobe Bryant (left) scored 60 or more points in six different games during his 20-year career.

Bird hit his 16th shot. He raised his finger in the air to celebrate his third straight victory.

In 2006, Kobe Bryant treated Lakers fans to one of the greatest scoring performances in basketball history. That night, Bryant finished with 81 points in a Lakers victory over the Toronto Raptors. The game stands as the second-highest point total for a player in a game in the history of the NBA. In 1962, Wilt Chamberlain scored 100 points in a game for the Philadelphia Warriors.

In addition to winning the 2024 NBA Finals, the Boston Celtics were the league's best team in the regular season. Jaylen Brown, Jayson Tatum, Derrick White, and Kristaps Porziņģis each won the Eastern Conference Player of the Week award that year. It was the first time any team in the league had four different players win the award in a single season.

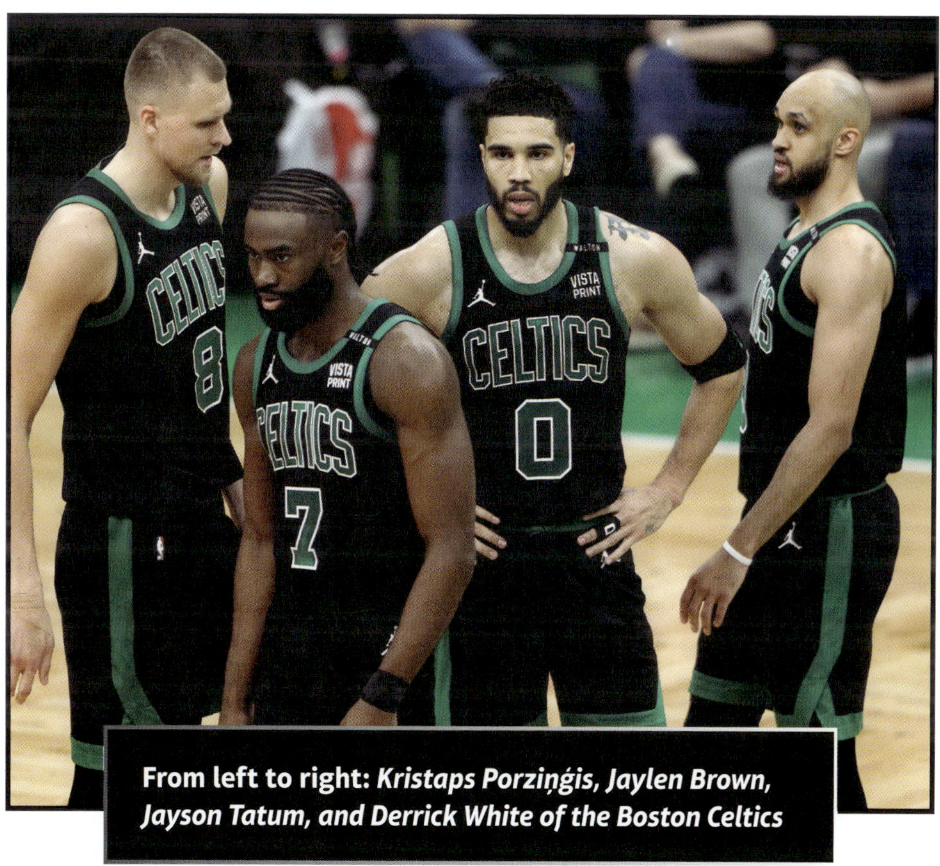

From left to right: ***Kristaps Porziņģis, Jaylen Brown, Jayson Tatum, and Derrick White of the Boston Celtics***

CHAPTER 3

Bill Russell shoots the ball. He finished his Celtics career with 14,522 points, the eighth-most in team history.

TALENTED TEAMMATES

Center Bill Russell led the Celtics to 11 NBA titles. He won the NBA's MVP award five times. Only Kareem Abdul-Jabbar has won more with six. Russell is widely considered one of the greatest defensive players in NBA history. He ranks second all-time in rebounds. Russell also served as the Celtics' head coach for three seasons and led the team to two NBA titles.

Together, Kareem Abdul-Jabbar and Magic Johnson

led the Lakers to five NBA titles between 1980 and 1988. Abdul-Jabbar ranks second all-time in scoring, with 38,387 points during his NBA career. His six NBA MVP awards may never be matched. He was an NBA All-Star 19 times.

Johnson won three NBA MVP awards and is the NBA's career leader in assists per game with 11.2. Johnson was chosen as an NBA All-Star 12 times. He remains one of the most popular and beloved players in NBA history.

Celtics great Larry Bird led Boston to three NBA titles during the 1980s. Like his rival Magic Johnson, Bird won three

Kareem Abdul-Jabbar averaged 24.6 points per game during his 20-year career.

Larry Bird shoots over two Lakers defenders, including longtime rival Magic Johnson (right).

NBA MVP awards during his career and was a 12-time All-Star. Bird played during a time when the three-point shot was less common. But he was one of the earliest players to regularly take and make long-range three-pointers.

After winning NBA championships with two other teams, superstar LeBron James joined the Lakers in 2018. He led the Lakers to their 17th NBA title in 2020. James is the NBA's all-time leading scorer, with more than 42,000 points and counting. He has won four MVP awards in his career and has been an All-Star 21 times.

CHECK IT OUT

After winning six NBA titles with the Chicago Bulls, coach Phil Jackson led the Lakers to five championships from 2000 to 2010. His 11 total wins are the most for a coach in NBA history.

During the 2024–2025 season, Luka Dončić joined the Lakers in a trade that shocked the NBA. Dončić had played six seasons with the Dallas Mavericks. He was the NBA's top scorer in 2023–2024 and has been an All-Star five times. Dončić helped the Mavericks reach the NBA Finals in 2024 and led his team in points, rebounds, and assists.

Some fans think LeBron James is the best player in NBA history.

The Boston Celtics are led by a powerful duo of skilled players, Jaylen Brown and Jayson Tatum. Tatum is a six-time All-Star who has been part of the All-NBA team five times. Brown is a four-time All-Star who has averaged more than 20 points per game six times in his career. Together, Brown and Tatum led the Celtics to the NBA title in 2024, and Brown won the NBA Finals MVP award.

With Jayson Tatum (left) and Jaylen Brown (right) leading the team, Boston has a shot at winning more NBA titles in the future.

CHAPTER 4

The Lakers and Celtics played their 301st regular-season game on January 23, 2025. The Lakers won 117–96.

CHOOSE YOUR CHAMPION

Now that we've learned more about the Lakers and Celtics, which team comes out on top? There's no such thing as a right or wrong answer. Different people will have different opinions. Fans of each team will almost certainly say their team is the best.

The Lakers have the edge in total playoff appearances with 65, while the Celtics have made the playoffs 62 times. The Lakers have also reached the Finals 32 times, more than the Celtics' 23 Finals trips. But Boston has won the NBA title 18 times. The Lakers have won only 17 times.

Both teams have had some of the greatest athletes to ever play the game. Nineteen Celtics players are part of the Basketball Hall of Fame. Eighteen Lakers players have earned the same honor.

The deciding factor in this smackdown is their record against each other. The teams have played 302 games in the regular season, with the Celtics winning 167 times. They've

Leon Powe (left) and Pau Gasol go for the ball during the 2008 NBA Finals.

Jayson Tatum led the Celtics in points per game during the 2024–2025 season with 26.8.

also matched up 12 times in the NBA Finals, and the Celtics have won nine of those series. This gives the Celtics the edge in this incredibly close smackdown.

What do you think? Do you agree the Celtics are the best? Think about why or why not and make your own pick!

SMACKDOWN TIMELINE

BOSTON CELTICS

1946 The Boston Celtics begin their first season.

1957 The Celtics win their first title under coach Red Auerbach, defeating the St. Louis Hawks in the Finals.

1966 Boston wins its eighth championship in a row, setting an NBA record.

1969 In his last season, Bill Russell leads the Celtics to the team's 11th championship.

1984 Larry Bird wins his first NBA MVP award.

1984 The Celtics defeat the Lakers in a thrilling seven-game NBA Finals, winning the 15th title in team history.

2008 Led by their big three of Kevin Garnett, Paul Pierce, and Ray Allen, the Celtics win their 17th title.

2024 Boston beats the Dallas Mavericks in the NBA Finals and earns its 18th title, passing the Lakers for the most in NBA history.

2025 Jayson Tatum injures his leg in the playoffs and the Celtics lose to the New York Knicks.

LOS ANGELES LAKERS

1947 The Lakers begin play in Minneapolis, Minnesota.

1949 Led by George Mikan, the Lakers win their first NBA championship.

1960 The Lakers move to Los Angeles.

1980 Stars Magic Johnson and Kareem Abdul-Jabbar lead the Lakers to their first title together.

1985 For the first time in their history, the Lakers defeat the Celtics in the NBA Finals.

2000 Shaquille O'Neal and Kobe Bryant win their first of three titles together.

2008 Kobe Bryant wins his first NBA MVP award.

2020 LeBron James leads the Lakers to their most recent title.

2025 The Lakers trade for superstar Luka Dončić.

GLOSSARY

All-Star: a player chosen as one of the best in the league to compete in a game against other top players

assist: a pass that leads directly to a basket

center: a player who usually stays close to the basket and the middle of the court

forward: a player who usually plays near the basket

free throw: an open shot taken from behind a set line after a foul by an opponent

guard: a player who usually plays away from the basket

Hall of Fame: a museum in Springfield, Illinois, that honors the best players in basketball history

jump shot: a shot made by jumping into the air and releasing the ball at the top of the jump

NBA Finals: a series of games between the winner of the NBA's Eastern and Western Conferences to decide each year's NBA champion

rebound: grabbing and controlling the ball after a missed shot

rivalry: when two players or teams compete for the same goal

LEARN MORE

Boston Celtics Facts for Kids
https://kids.kiddle.co/Boston_Celtics

Donnelly, Patrick. *Los Angeles Lakers*. SportsZone: Minneapolis, 2023.

Kjartansson, Kjartan Atli. *Legends of the NBA*. Abbeville Kids: New York, 2022.

Kobe Bryant
https://www.ducksters.com/sports/kobe_bryant.php

National Basketball Association (NBA)
https://kids.britannica.com/students/article/National-Basketball-Association-NBA/624441

Stewart, Mark. *The Boston Celtics*. Norwood House Press: Chicago, 2025.

INDEX

PHOTO ACKNOWLEDGMENTS

Image credits: Christian Petersen/Getty Images, p. 4; Christian Petersen/Getty Images, p. 6; Paul Kitagaki Jr./ZUMAPRESS/Newscom, p. 7; Melissa Tamez/Icon Sportswire/Getty Images, p. 7; Marty Jean-Louis/Sipa USA/Newscom, p. 7; Bettmann Archive/Getty Images, p. 8; Focus on Sport/Getty Images, p. 9; Focus on Sport/Getty Images, p. 10; Minnesota Historical Society/Corbis/Getty Images, p. 11; Jeff Lewis/Icon SMI 910/Newscom, p. 12; AFP/Getty Images, p. 13; AP Photo/AP Newsroom, p. 14; Ronald L. Mrowiec/Sporting News Archive/Getty Images, p. 15; Bob Riha Jr./Archive Photos/Getty Images, p. 16; Jim Zerschling/Photo Researchers History/Archive Photos/Getty Images, p. 17; Jeff Lewis/Icon SMI 910/Newscom, p. 18; Adam Glanzman/Getty Images, p. 19; Bettmann/Getty Images, p. 20; Focus on Sport/Getty Images, p. 21; Rick Stewart/Allsport/Hulton Archive, p. 22; Ronald Martinez/Getty Images, p. 23; Adam Glanzman/Getty Images, p. 24; Harry How/Getty Images, p. 25; Stuart Cahill/MediaNews Group/Boston Herald via Getty Images/Getty Images, p. 26, Elsa/Getty Images, p. 27.

Cover: Marty Jean-Louis/Sipa USA/Newscom; Melissa Tamez/Icon Sportswire/Newscom; Melissa Tamez/Icon Sportswire/Newscom.